First Facts®

U.S. NATIONAL PARKS FIELD GUIDES

GLACIER
NATIONAL PARK

by Katie Parker

PEBBLE
a capstone imprint

First Facts Books are published by Pebble,
1710 Roe Crest Drive, North Mankato, Minnesota 56003
www.mycapstone.com

Library of Congress Cataloging-in-Publication Data is available
on the Library of Congress website.
ISBN 978-1-9771-0354-3 (library binding)
ISBN 978-1-9771-0524-0 (paperback)
ISBN 978-1-9771-0361-1 (ebook pdf)

Editorial Credits:
Anna Butzer, editor
Juliette Peters, designer
Tracy Cummins, media researcher
Kathy McColley, production specialist

Photo Credits:
Alamy: Don Geyer, 15 Top; Capstone: Eric Gohl, 7 Top, 9 Bottom,
13 Bottom, 17 Bottom; Getty Images: Danita Delimont, 18, Feng
Wei Photography, 19; Newscom: Danita Delimont Photography,
14 Bottom; Shutterstock: Aliaksei Baturytski, 21 Middle, Andrey
Tarantin, 2–3, aprilwilsonphotos, 3 Top, Cat_arch_angel, Design
Element, chamski, 21 Top, Christine Krahl, Design Element,
Dan Breckwoldt, Back Cover, Cover Top, Dean Fikar, 15 Bottom,
Frank Fichtmueller, 3 Middle, Frontpage, 9 Top, Hugo Brizard -
YouGoPhoto, 12–13, Jason Patrick Ross, 10, Jeremy Christensen,
17 Top, kan_khampanya, Cover Bottom Middle, Kevin Wells
Photography, 5 Top, lconti, 7 Bottom, maelm, 12 Bottom, mattymeis,
20–21, mlorenz, 22–23, 24, Nina B, 3 Bottom, NottomanV1, Design
Element, PARADOX_M, 11, Pung, 5 Bottom, Sean Xu, 13 Top,
Tom Reichner, Cover Bottom Right, 21 Bottom, Tricia Daniel, 6,
tusharkoley, 16–17, Vaclav Sebek, 1, Vlad Klok, Design Element,
Wildnerdpix, Cover Bottom Left, 8–9, Wikimedia: By Tyrooooone -
Own work, CC BY-SA 3.0, https://commons.wikimedia.org/w/index.
php?curid=28180106, 14 Top

Printed and bound in the USA.
1335

Table of Contents

Welcome to Glacier National Park

Where can you stand with one foot on either side of the **Continental Divide**? This spot is found in **Glacier** National Park.

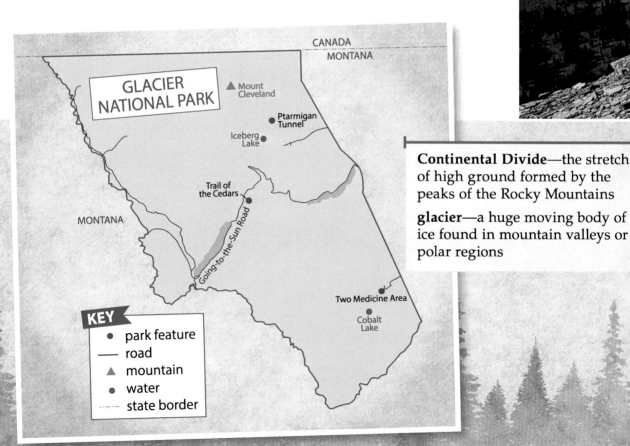

CANADA
MONTANA

GLACIER NATIONAL PARK

▲ Mount Cleveland

Ptarmigan Tunnel

Iceberg Lake

Trail of the Cedars

Going-to-the-Sun Road

MONTANA

Two Medicine Area

Cobalt Lake

KEY
- • park feature
- — road
- ▲ mountain
- • water
- ‑‑‑ state border

Continental Divide—the stretch of high ground formed by the peaks of the Rocky Mountains

glacier—a huge moving body of ice found in mountain valleys or polar regions

Continental Divide, Montana

This giant park in Montana once had more than 150 glaciers. Only 26 remain today. The other glaciers melted away. When glaciers melt, they slowly move. Over time, they carve valleys in the mountains. The land in Glacier National Park looks different today than it did 100 years ago.

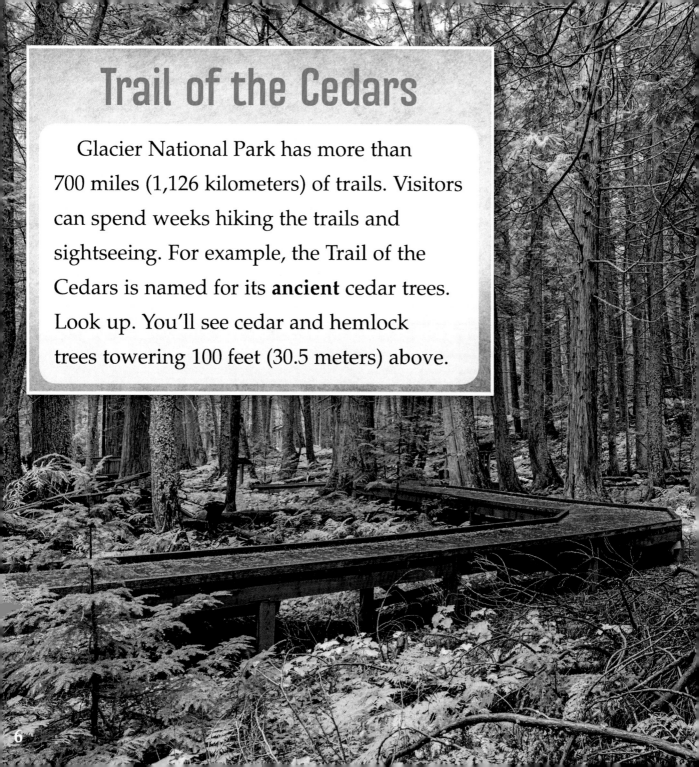

Trail of the Cedars

Glacier National Park has more than 700 miles (1,126 kilometers) of trails. Visitors can spend weeks hiking the trails and sightseeing. For example, the Trail of the Cedars is named for its **ancient** cedar trees. Look up. You'll see cedar and hemlock trees towering 100 feet (30.5 meters) above.

Trail of the Cedars

Haystack Creek

Going-to-the-Sun Road

Avalanche Creek

KEY
—— Trail of the Cedars
—— road
—— river

FACT: On your hike you'll pass through a rain forest. It is one of the only rain forests in the world that isn't near an ocean. The wet weather helps trees grow tall. It keeps them safe from forest fires.

ancient—from a long time ago

Hike to Cobalt Lake

Many visitors hike the rough, 11-mile (17.7 km) trail to Cobalt Lake. This trail is steep in places and there is not much shade.

FACT: What is the most dangerous part of Glacier National Park? Mama bears? Hungry mountain lions? The answer is wet rocks. More people get hurt slipping on wet rocks than from other park dangers.

∧ Two Medicine Lake and Rising Wolf Mountain

^ moose

There are many moose sightings on this trail. Moose are often seen near the ponds at Paradise Point. Visitors will also see Two Medicine Lake and Rising Wolf Mountain from Paradise Point.

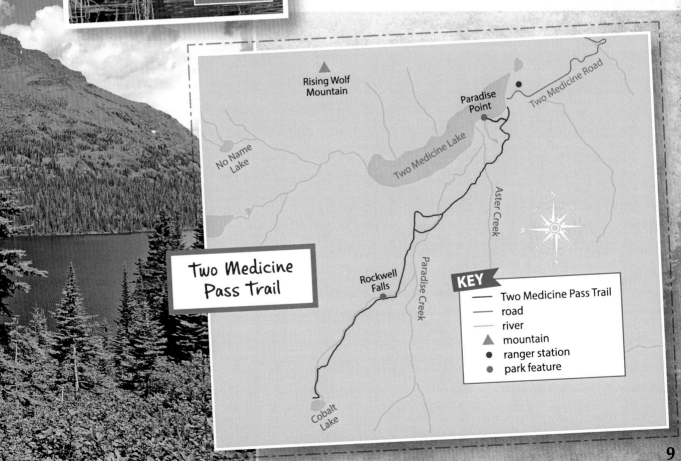

Two Medicine Pass Trail

Rising Wolf Mountain

Paradise Point

Two Medicine Road

No Name Lake

Two Medicine Lake

Aster Creek

Paradise Creek

Rockwell Falls

Cobalt Lake

KEY
— Two Medicine Pass Trail
— road
— river
▲ mountain
● ranger station
● park feature

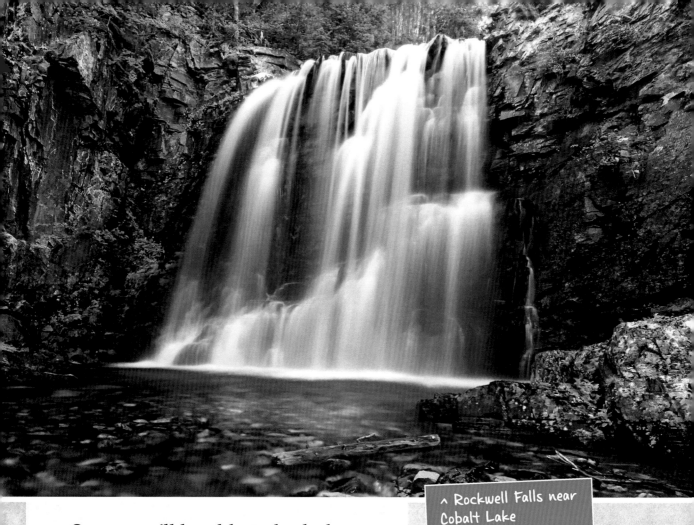

∧ Rockwell Falls near Cobalt Lake

Soon you'll be able to look down from Two Medicine Pass Trail. There sits Cobalt Lake in a u-shaped **valley**. You can climb down and stick your feet in the water.

valley—an area of low ground between two hills, usually containing a river

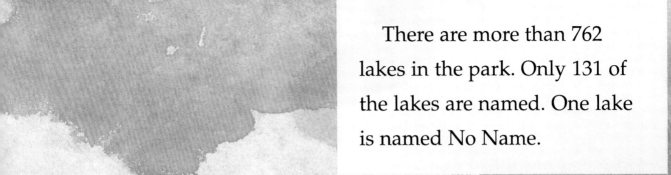

There are more than 762 lakes in the park. Only 131 of the lakes are named. One lake is named No Name.

∧ No Name Lake

Iceberg Lake Trail

Cobalt Lake is in the southern end of the park. Travel north and you'll find Iceberg Lake. You won't want to dip your toes into this lake. All year long, Iceberg Lake has many large sheets of ice floating in it. Brrrr!

FACT: Trails in this area are often closed because of grizzly bears. Hike in large groups and make lots of noise. And make sure you carry bear spray!

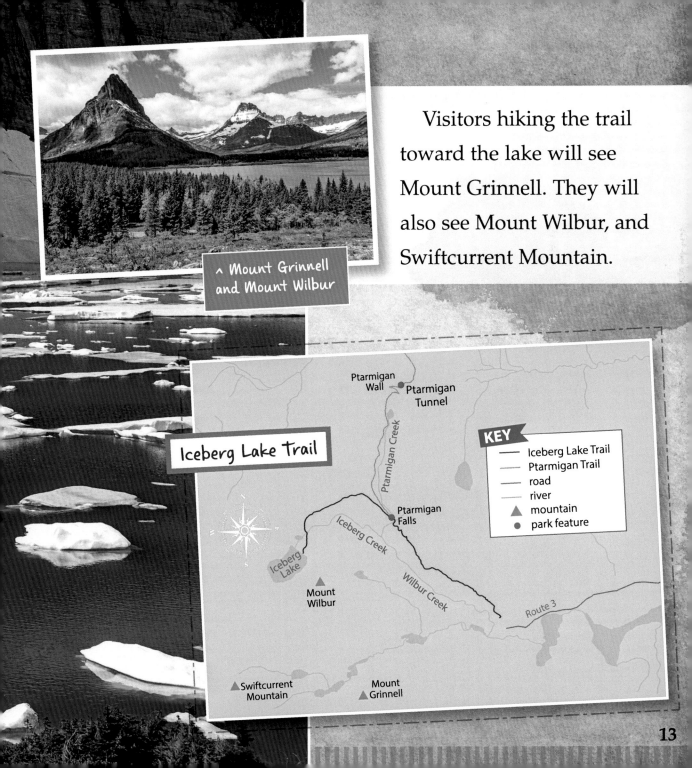

Visitors hiking the trail toward the lake will see Mount Grinnell. They will also see Mount Wilbur, and Swiftcurrent Mountain.

∧ Mount Grinnell and Mount Wilbur

Iceberg Lake Trail

Ptarmigan Wall

Ptarmigan Tunnel

Ptarmigan Creek

Ptarmigan Falls

Iceberg Creek

Wilbur Creek

Route 3

Iceberg Lake

Mount Wilbur

Swiftcurrent Mountain

Mount Grinnell

KEY

— Iceberg Lake Trail
— Ptarmigan Trail
— road
— river
▲ mountain
● park feature

^ Ptarmigan Tunnel

Ptarmigan Tunnel was built so hikers could cross between two valleys. In 1930 workers began creating a tunnel on both sides of the mountain. They used jackhammers and dynamite to break away at the rock.

Ptarmigan Wall >

Travel through the Ptarmigan Tunnel and discover deep drops and narrow paths. Visitors will also discover the Ptarmigan Wall Goat Trail. It was made by mountain goats along the mountain's side.

^ Ptarmigan Wall trail

^ Ptarmigan Lake as seen from the top of Ptarmigan Trail

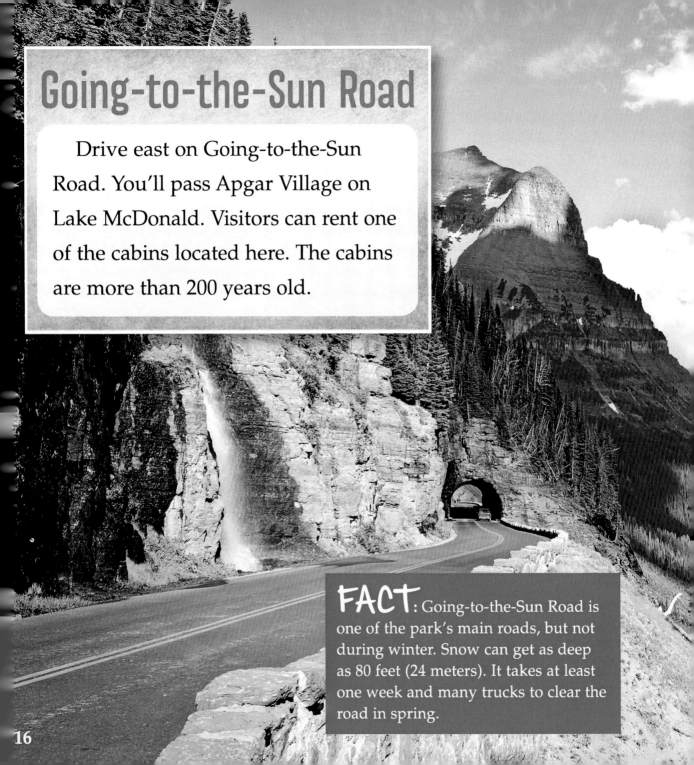

Going-to-the-Sun Road

Drive east on Going-to-the-Sun Road. You'll pass Apgar Village on Lake McDonald. Visitors can rent one of the cabins located here. The cabins are more than 200 years old.

FACT: Going-to-the-Sun Road is one of the park's main roads, but not during winter. Snow can get as deep as 80 feet (24 meters). It takes at least one week and many trucks to clear the road in spring.

Hike up and down steep trails and rocky hills. Then stroll through **alpine** meadows with the smell and sights of wildflowers. Discover tall, white flowers called beargrass. Bears collect the soft flower to make their dens cozier.

alpine—having to do with high mountains

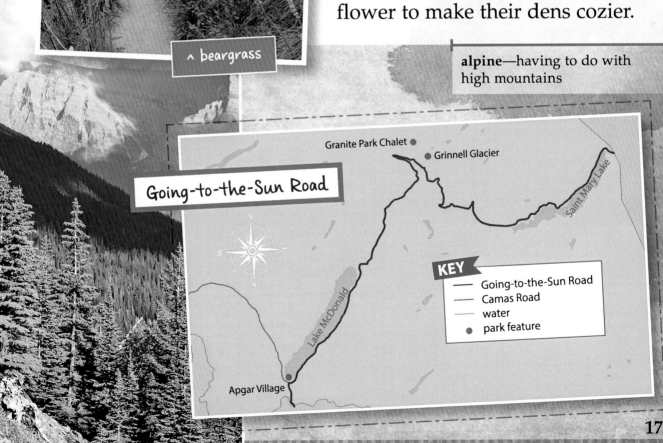

Going-to-the-Sun Road

Granite Park Chalet ●

● Grinnell Glacier

Saint Mary Lake

Lake McDonald

Apgar Village ●

KEY
— Going-to-the-Sun Road
— Camas Road
— water
● park feature

Spend the night at the **rustic** Granite Park **Chalet**. In the morning you can head back to your car. Or you can travel deeper into the park. The Chalet marks the beginning of many trails in Glacier National Park.

rustic—simple and useful, not at all fancy

chalet—a wooden house or cottage

Mount Cleveland

FACT: The tallest mountain in Glacier National Park is Mount Cleveland. It's almost 10,500 feet (3,200 m) high. People often hike up the mountain and camp along the way.

A Great Treasure

As its glaciers shrink, interest in the park grows. The number of visitors to Glacier National Park has never been higher. About 2 million people visit the park each year. They come to see the glaciers, mountains, lakes, and wildlife. Glacier National Park is one of North America's great treasures.

Grinnell Glacier ^

< red fox

^ bighorn sheep

< white-tailed ptarmigan

FACT: There are over 2,000 species of wildflowers in Glacier National Park. More than 260 kinds of birds and 70 kinds of mammals live in the park.

Glossary

alpine (AL-pyn)—having to do with high mountains

ancient (AYN-shunt)—from a long time ago

chalet (SHAL-ay)—a wooden house or cottage

Continental Divide (kahn-tuh-NEN-tuhl duh-VYD)—the stretch of high ground formed by the peaks of the Rocky Mountains

glacier (GLAY-shur)—a huge moving body of ice found in mountain valleys or polar regions

rustic (RUHSS-tik)—simple and useful, not at all fancy

valley (VAL-ee)—an area of land between two hills, usually containing a river

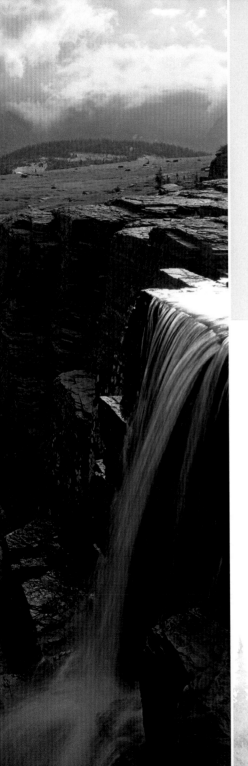

Read More

Hansen, Grace. *Glacier National Park.* National Parks. Minneapolis: Abdo Kids, 2018.

Higgins, Nadia. *Welcome to Glacier National Park.* National Parks. Mankato, MN: Childs World, 2018.

Mattern, Joanne. *Glacier National Park.* Rookie National Parks. New York: Children's Press, 2018.

Internet Sites

Use FactHound to find Internet sites related to this book:

Visit *www.facthound.com*

Just type in 9781977103543 and go.

 Check out projects, games and lots more at
www.capstonekids.com

Critical Thinking Questions

1. What items should you bring when you're going for a day hike in Glacier National Park?

2. Why might it be important to wear waterproof shoes to the park?

3. Look at the trail maps in the book. How can you use maps to plan a hike?

Index